# All About
# Madam C. J. Walker

A'Lelia Bundles

## BLUE RIVER PRESS

Indianapolis, Indiana

All About Madam C. J. Walker
Copyright © 2017 by A'Lelia Bundles

Published by Blue River Press
Indianapolis, Indiana
www.brpressbooks.com

Distributed by Cardinal Publishers Group
A Tom Doherty Company, Inc.
www.cardinalpub.com

ISBN: 978-1-68157-093-8

Author: A'Lelia Bundles
Editor: Dani McCormick
Interior Illustrator: Kirsten Halvorsen
Book Design: Dave Reed
Cover Artist: Jennifer Mujezinovic
Cover Design: David Miles

Printed in the United States of America

23 22 21 20 19 18 17      1 2 3 4 5 6 7

# Contents

# All About
# Madam C. J. Walker

# Preface

Madam C. J. Walker was one of the most successful American businesswomen of the early twentieth century. She is remembered as an entrepreneur and pioneer of the modern hair care industry. She also made her mark as a philanthropist, a patron of the arts, and a political activist who spoke out against racial injustice.

Walker had very humble beginnings. She was born Sarah Breedlove on a plantation in Delta, Louisiana in 1867, two years after the end of the Civil War. Her parents, Owen and Minerva Breedlove, died before she was seven years old. As a child, she had almost no formal education.

She married at a very young age and was widowed when she was twenty. In 1888, she and her three-year old daughter Lelia moved to St. Louis where her older brothers were barbers.

She joined St. Paul African Methodist Episcopal Church and met very kind female church members, who helped her adjust to the city. She never forgot their generosity; the example they set became a model for her own philanthropy.

Walker worked as a laundress for many years and made very little money, but she was determined to give her daughter more opportunities than she had had.

There is an old saying that "necessity is the mother of invention." This certainly was true for Walker. She was losing her hair because of a severe scalp infection and was desperate for a cure for her bald spots.

She often said that her formula came to her in a dream after she prayed for a solution. But she also took advice from others until she finally came up with the right combination of ingredients.

In 1906, after she married her third husband, Charles Joseph Walker, she began calling herself

Madam C. J. Walker. She also began selling an ointment called Madam Walker's Wonderful Hair Grower that became very popular.

In 1908, she opened Lelia College of Beauty Culture to train sales agents to use her products. In 1910 she moved to Indianapolis, Indiana where she built a factory. By 1911, her business was already so successful that she was able to make a $1,000 contribution to the local Young Men's Christian Association (YMCA) for a new building.

She moved to Harlem in 1916 and became involved in political activities including the National Association for the Advancement of Colored People's (NAACP) anti-lynching campaign. In 1917, she hosted one of the first large gatherings of American businesswomen when she convened her Madam C. J. Walker Beauty Culturists Union in Philadelphia.

Walker developed an international business with customers all over the United States, Central America, and the Caribbean. She provided jobs for African American women; instead of being hired by someone else as maids, laundresses, and farmworkers, they were able to work for themselves.

When Walker died in 1919, she left more than $100,000 to political causes, organizations, and educational institutions.

In 1998, she became the twenty-first African American to be featured in the United States Postal Service's Black Heritage Series. There also are two National Historic Landmarks—the Madam Walker Theatre Center, a cultural arts center in Indianapolis; and Villa Lewaro, her Westchester County, New York mansion—that bear her name.

More than a century after she founded her company, the Madam C. J. Walker Beauty Culture line of products is manufactured by Sundial Brands and sold throughout the United States.

At the root of Walker's success was her belief in her high-quality products, her gift for market-ing, and her ability to lead and inspire others.

# Chapter 1
## Free Born Baby

Baby Sarah brought so much joy to the Breedlove family. Born just two days before Christmas in 1867, she was an early holiday gift. Her parents, Owen and Minerva Anderson Breedlove, smiled at her chocolate brown skin and soft coils of black hair. Inside their drafty cabin in Delta, Louisiana, they celebrated the arrival of their first freeborn child.

By candlelight, her siblings Louvenia, Owen Jr., Alexander, and James all looked at their little sister with high hopes. Like their parents, they had come into the world as enslaved people. Until the Civil War ended in April 1865, they had been owned by Robert W. Burney and worked on his cotton plantation in Madison Parish.

Under the American system of slavery, they were not paid for their labor. Like four million other human beings of African descent, they could not come and go as they pleased. They did not have the same legal rights and privileges as free white Americans. But that did not stop them from having dreams and wishes for themselves and their children.

After Emancipation, the Breedloves were no longer enslaved, but they had no savings and owned no property. With a young family to rear, Owen and Minerva realized it would not be easy to start over in a new place where they had no friends. Because they were used to living and working on the Burney plantation, they decided it was more practical to stay.

They continued to farm the same land, but now they were called sharecroppers instead of

Sarah was born in the Breedlove family's one-room cabin in Delta, Louisiana.

slaves. At the end of each harvest, they turned over all the cotton they had picked to Mr. Burney so he could sell it to a cotton gin. Eventually, the raw cotton ended up at a mill where it was woven into fabric and sewn into shirts, dresses, sheets, and linens.

Many other people made money from the cotton the Breedloves had picked, but they received only a few dollars for several months of hard work. By the time they paid for cabin rent, cottonseed, and other expenses, they always owed more than they had earned. It was a vicious cycle that never allowed them to turn a profit.

Even little girls and boys had to work in the fields. Sarah learned to pull weeds and clean the cotton bolls. She planted corn and cabbage in the family garden and tended the chickens. They all worked from sun up to sun down in the steamy Louisiana sun.

Each year they prayed for their lives to get better, but it was hard to be optimistic. Although they now were free American citizens, they saw little difference in their daily lives.

Sarah and her siblings worked as sharecroppers on a cotton plantation picking cotton bolls.

Before the Civil War, Madison Parish had been one of the richest farming communities in the South. Delta was located on the western side of the Mississippi River across from Vicksburg, Mississippi. There was no bridge across the river, so a ferry transported livestock, cotton, corn, lumber, clothing, and other items from one shore to the other. The products were then loaded onto train cars and shipped to the eastern and western United States.

Delta's strategic position on a waterway had made it a wartime target. During an 1864 battle called the Siege of Vicksburg, Union Army soldiers destroyed farms, burned houses and barns, killed animals, and took other valuables that belonged to Confederacy sympathizers like the Burneys.

During the Civil War Sarah's parents witnessed a battle called the Siege of Vicksburg.

After the war, plantation owners still needed thousands of workers. As a result, black residents like the Breedloves outnumbered white residents by ten to one in northern Louisiana. Those numbers translated into political power after the passage of three Amendments to the United States Constitution. The Thirteenth Amendment abolished slavery. The Fourteenth Amendment guaranteed citizenship for newly freed people. The Fifteenth Amendment granted black men, like Sarah's father and older brothers, the right to vote. American women would not get the right to vote until 1920.

White landowners did not want black citizens to vote or make progress, but the Breedloves were proud that Reverend Curtis Pollard, their family minister, had been elected as a senator in the Louisiana state legislature.

At church on Sundays, Sarah sat on a bench next to her friend Celeste Hawkins. After the service, they caught crawfish in the nearby bayous and enjoyed fish fries and picnics. When they jumped rope, they recited rhymes and practiced their ABCs.

Owen and Minerva craved education for Sarah and her siblings. Literacy was a symbol of freedom because laws before the Civil War had made it illegal for black people to read and write. Slave owners were afraid they would make plans to escape if they were literate.

Sarah and her friends enjoyed jumping rope at church picnics.

Public schools were rare in Louisiana, especially in rural areas like Madison Parish where the local governments would not fund them. It was another way to control the black workers and their families. When churches organized classes, racist terrorist groups called the Ku Klux Klan (KKK) and the Knights of the White Camellia burned the buildings. They even murdered black teachers and students.

With so much work to do in the fields, there was little time to study and little time to rest. Sarah stayed busy helping her mother and sister, Louvenia, with laundry and other chores. At the time, no houses had electricity, and the electric washing machine had not been invented. Instead, they scrubbed clothes by hand on washboards in creeks and large wooden tubs. Wet sheets and

Sarah usually washed clothes by the creek,
but sometimes her family washed them in tubs instead

linen tablecloths were very heavy and hard for one person to lift.

Although the work was difficult, Sarah was always happy to be with her mother. She especially enjoyed hearing the women and older girls sing. Their harmony and rhythm helped them forget the drudgery. Sometimes when their voices blended with horns from the passing steamboats and train whistles at Delta depot, Sarah imagined herself traveling to far away places.

Long days, poor diet, and lack of proper medical care took a toll on the Breedloves and other sharecropping families. Minor ailments easily turned into major illnesses without medicine and rest. When Sarah was six years old, her mother died when a cholera epidemic struck the community. Within a few months, her father remarried, but he, too, died before her seventh birthday. The exact causes of their deaths will never be known.

Now an orphan, Sarah had no choice but to move in with her sister. She missed her parents, and Louvenia was too busy looking after her own little boy, Willie, to pay much attention to Sarah. Louvenia's husband, Jesse Powell, was very mean to Sarah and made her feel unwelcome.

Life in Delta had gotten dangerous and violent. During the presidential election of 1876, the KKK tampered with ballots and attacked black residents who tried to vote. They were determined to take away the civil and political

Yellow Fever affected many people in the late 1870's, from Delta, Mississippi to Memphis, Tennessee

rights that African Americans had gained during Reconstruction.

Two years later, just before Sarah turned eleven years old, yellow fever—a disease spread by infected mosquitoes—swept through the region. More than 3,000 people died. To make matters worse, bad weather and insects called boll weevils destroyed the cotton crop. With no cotton to pick, there was no way to make money.

Although Reverend Pollard had lost his state senate seat in 1876, he remained a leader in the community. Now that the KKK was in power, he could see that black people would not be treated fairly. Political violence and racial discrimination had become so horrible that he began to encourage members of his congregation to leave Louisiana.

Sarah's older brothers Alexander, Owen, and James listened to Reverend Pollard's advice. Because they believed they could not make a decent living in Louisiana, they decided to move to St. Louis, a prosperous town farther north on the Mississippi River. They joined thousands of other migrants who hoped to improve their lives. When they arrived in the Missouri city in 1880, they worked as laborers. Soon, they began to learn the barbering trade.

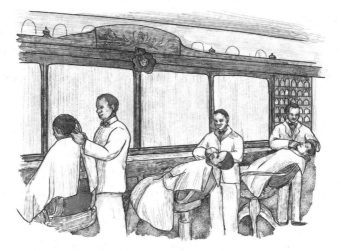

Sarah's older brothers wanted to own a fancy barbershop

With her brothers gone, Sarah was lonelier than ever. She also was afraid of her brother-in-law, Jesse. To escape his abuse, she married Moses McWilliams when she was fourteen. She later said she made her decision at such a young age to "get a home of my own."

Like Sarah, Moses did not have much formal education. He found work loading cotton bales onto boats, repairing train tracks, and harvesting cotton. Sarah picked cotton, too, and continued to wash clothes to earn money.

On June 6, 1885, when Sarah was seventeen, she and Moses had a daughter, whom they named Lelia. Having her own family made Sarah happier than she had been in many years, but that happiness lasted only a short time. Soon after Lelia's second birthday, Moses died. There is no death certificate, so the cause of his death is not known.

At twenty years old, Sarah was suddenly a widow and single mother. She refused to return to her sister and brother-in-law's home. Instead, she mustered all her courage and vowed to join her brothers in St. Louis. She had heard that she could get work washing clothes. She also had heard that there were public schools for her child.

With Lelia holding onto her skirt and with her few belongings wrapped into a bundle, Sarah boarded a northbound steamboat. She was not sure what she would find in Missouri, but she knew she could not stay in Mississippi.

Sarah and her husband, Moses McWilliams,
welcomed their daughter, Lelia in June 1885.

# Chapter 2
# Dreaming of a Better Life

Sarah stood on the steps outside her rickety rooming house waiting for Lelia to get home from school. Their afternoon hug was the best part of her day.

She just spent several hours in the backyard washing clothes in a wooden tub. Knowing her daughter was getting an education made every sacrifice worthwhile. Still, as she'd looked at piles of dirty laundry that morning, she had fears and doubts about the future.

She later told the New York Times that she had wondered, "What are you going to do when you grow old and your back gets stiff? Who is going to take care of your little girl?"

"This set me to thinking, but with all my thinking, I couldn't see how I, a poor washerwoman, was going to better my condition."

St. Louis was America's sixth largest city
when Sarah arrived in 1888.

Even with these worries, she knew the move to
St. Louis had been for the best. Vicksburg would
always be a small town with little opportunity,
but St. Louis was a metropolis with almost half
a million people. Downtown streets bustled
with trolleys and horse-drawn buggies. Migrants
from the South like Sarah hurried past the same
fancy department store window displays and
tall buildings as Missouri natives, transplanted
Easterners, and European immigrants. Along
the riverfront, tons of cargo were loaded and
unloaded every day. Near the train station on

Market Street, gamblers gathered in saloons and pool halls. German musicians entertained in neighborhood bier gardens, while Scott Joplin's ragtime tunes drew crowds to Tom Turpin's Rosebud Café.

By the 1890s, the city was home to Anheuser-Busch, the nation's largest beer brewery, and Liggett & Myers, a major tobacco processor. These companies and dozens of other factories were eager to hire white men. But the dirtiest, most dangerous jobs went to black men, if they were hired at all. Black women were wanted only for menial, poorly paid housekeeping tasks.

When Sarah and Lelia first arrived in St. Louis in 1888, they lived with one of her brothers, who helped as much as he could. Soon Sarah found work as a maid. But the long hours made it hard for her to get home every night to care for Lelia. Often her only day off was Sunday.

Because there were no daycare centers for children of working mothers, she was forced to leave Lelia at the St. Louis Colored Orphans Home during the week. It broke her heart to be away from her child, but the women who founded the home were very understanding and helpful.

They could see that she was trying to improve her life. It was not long before Sarah was able to leave her job as a maid and begin washing and ironing. These were tasks she could do at home. That freedom gave her more time to spend with Lelia.

Every Sunday, they attended St. Paul African Methodist Episcopal (AME) Church, one of the city's oldest black churches. Just as the women at the orphanage had noticed Sarah's ambition, so did the women of St. Paul.

Sarah sang in the choir on Sundays at
St. Paul African Methodist Episcopal Church.

One member in particular, Jessie Batts Robinson, got to know Sarah during the year when Lelia was a student in her elementary school class. Jessie's husband, Christopher K. Robinson, owned the *Clarion* newspaper. They both were influential officers in a national fraternal organization called the Knights of Pythias.

They took a particular interest in Sarah and invited her to their home. Jessie became her mentor. She urged her to join the choir and the Mite Missionary Society, where Sarah was exposed to women with more education and sophistication.

Sarah was grateful for their encouragement. Because of them, she learned to read and write and to have new dreams and goals. She counted her blessings.

But then Sarah had more setbacks. In 1893, her eldest brother, Alexander, died. He always had been the family leader so his death was a major blow.

That same year, several banks and businesses failed. This caused a national financial crisis called the Panic of 1893. Wealthy people suffered, but poor, working people like Sarah had an even harder time.

In 1894, Sarah married a man named John Davis. She hoped they could build a life together and that he would help her raise her daughter. She soon realized she had made a mistake. Instead of helping with the rent and groceries, he spent his money on liquor and gambling. Some nights he did not come home. Other nights he would hit Sarah and threaten Lelia.

Before he came into their lives, Lelia had had perfect attendance at school. Now he was causing so many problems and so much turmoil that she often missed class. Education for Lelia was Sarah's most important goal at the time and she knew Davis was interfering.

She decided to leave him. Jessie Robinson and her church friends offered some help, but once again she was on her own.

Many of the missionary society's members were prominent, well-traveled women, who belonged to the National Association of Colored Women (NACW). In 1904, during the St. Louis World's Fair, more than 200 delegates came to the city from thirty-one states for the organization's biennial convention.

Sarah was not a member, but when the NACW held one of its sessions at St. Paul, she volunteered to assist. At the meetings, she listened to presentations about their work in orphanages, retirement homes, kindergartens, and clinics for tuberculosis patients. NACW president, Margaret Murray Washington—the wife of Tuskegee Institute founder Booker T. Washington—led them in discussions about women's suffrage and lynching. They also talked about segregated trains where white passengers were seated in comfortable and clean sections, but black passengers paid the same price for older, dirty cars. Sarah respected them even more after they voted to cancel their visit to the fairgrounds to protest because black workers and visitors had been mistreated.

Sarah helped with the NACW's annual meeting
which happened at the same time as the St. Louis World's Fair.

As Sarah watched the proceedings, she admired Mrs. Washington's poise and dignity. She could see the link between inner attitude and outward appearance. Good grooming reinforced self-confidence and vice versa.

She could not afford the expensive dresses worn by some of the delegates, but she took pride in her expertly laundered and carefully ironed clothes. No matter how nicely she dressed, though, she was embarrassed by her hair. She usually covered her head to hide the bald patches that showed her infected and inflamed scalp.

Margaret Murray Washington was president of the National Association of Colored Women, a civic organization that helped women and children.

It was a time when most Americans lived in homes without electricity, indoor bathtubs, or toilets. Whenever they wanted to bathe, they first had to pump water from outdoor wells, then boil it in large containers over open fires. That made the process so time-consuming and complicated that they might only take a bath once a week. They washed their hair even less often and sometimes not at all during the winter.

Sarah was desperate for a solution for her hair problems. She asked her brothers, who were barbers, for advice. She tried home remedies. She ordered some of the items she saw in black newspapers, but concoctions like Ford's Original Ozonized Ox Marrow and Kinkilla did more harm than good.

Sarah tried several ointments and shampoos because she was losing her hair.

After getting tips from her brothers and using products made by a local woman named Annie Pope-Turnbo, the sores on her scalp began to heal. Once the infection and the dandruff were gone, her hair began to grow back. She signed up as a sales agent for Pope-Turnbo's Poro Company.

She used the extra money to pay Lelia's tuition at Knoxville College in Tennessee. She also was able to afford to leave her second husband, John Davis, who drank too much liquor and was unfaithful.

With Lelia away at school and her marriage ended, Sarah had no reason to remain in St. Louis. Just as she had moved from Vicksburg to get a fresh start, she prepared to move again. This time she headed for Denver to join her widowed sister-in-law, Lucy Breedlove, and her four nieces.

Sarah no longer was a poor washerwoman with her arms buried in soapsuds. She now considered herself an entrepreneur with clear plans to improve her life.

Annie Pope-Turnbo created Poro cosmetics,
for which Sarah was a sales agent

# Chapter 3
# On the Road

Sarah stepped off the train at Denver's Union Depot eager for new opportunities. Colorado's mountains and wide blue skies astonished her. The crisp, dry air was a welcome change from St. Louis's pollution and steamy, summer heat.

The entire state population was only slightly larger than the population of the city of St. Louis. The small black community numbered fewer than 10,000 residents, but some early settlers had become very prosperous by running hotels, investing in silver mines, and buying real estate. Like the cattlemen, miners, and land speculators Sarah saw on the wide boulevards, she was ready to reinvent herself and find her fortune.

With her sister-in-law's help, she rented an attic room. Right away, she joined Shorter Chapel AME Church and volunteered with the Mite Missionary Society. To promote her hair growing work, she bought business cards and took out an ad in the *Colorado Statesmen*, a local black newspaper.

While she built her client base, Sarah supplemented her income by working as a cook for Edmund L. Scholtz, owner of the largest pharmacy west of the Mississippi River. Among the items he stocked was a scalp treatment and soap called Cuticura. He also used his pharmaceutical knowledge to make salves that healed skin ailments. When he saw Sarah selling Poro products, he let her know about other formulas that would help her achieve the same or similar results.

Sometimes she ran out of her Poro supply. At other times, the shipments were delayed or lost. In her frustration, she began experimenting with her own mixture. Sarah also had begun to have personal conflicts and business disagreements with Pope-Turnbo. She preferred being her own boss and resolved to keep testing her own ideas about sales and hair care.

Ever since arriving in Colorado, Sarah had been writing letters to Charles Joseph Walker, a close St. Louis friend, who sold newspaper advertisements and subscriptions. Their mutual interest in business soon turned to a mutual attraction beyond business. Walker, who was known to his friends as "C. J.," moved to Denver in late 1905. A few weeks later, on January 4, 1906, they were married in a friend's home.

C. J. Walker helped his new wife create advertisements for her new line of hair care products.

C. J. encouraged Sarah to continue tweaking the formula. She tested different combinations of coconut oil, beeswax, fragrance, and petrolatum, an ointment like Vaseline. The key ingredient was sulfur, a chemical element that had been used for thousands of years to heal skin infections like dandruff, eczema, and acne.

In Denver, Sarah married Charles Joseph "C. J." Walker
and began making her own
Madam Walker's Wonderful Hair Grower.

By now she had come to realize that her talents went beyond giving scalp treatments and grooming healthy hair. She had the kind of personality that allowed her to excel at marketing, promotion, public speaking, and teaching. She was helping other women become more confident. She was using the skills she had learned from watching the leaders of St. Paul's choir, the Mite Missionary Society, and the NACW.

In April 1906, Sarah made a bold business move by introducing her own product and a bold branding move by calling herself "*Madam C. J. Walker.*" The title before her name was intended to make customers think of Paris, the world's fashion and cosmetics capital, where married women were addressed as "Madame."

C. J. Walker helped Sarah design a very effective three-photo ad for the *Statesman*. In the center portrait, Sarah's hair was thin and patchy. To the left and to the right, her tresses were full, bushy, long, and healthy. The "before and after" images provided evidence that her Madam Walker's Wonderful Hair Grower worked.

Having transformed herself from a laundress to an entrepreneur in a few short years, she was her own best advertisement for success. Her weekly sales tripled, then quadrupled, then quintupled!

Madam Walker before and after her wonderful discovery.

Madam Walker's first ads were designed to show that her ointment had healed her scalp infections and helped her hair grow long.

With such a small black population, the newly named Madam C. J. Walker had quickly saturated Colorado's market. Once again, she was ready to relocate.

She persuaded Lelia, who was now twenty-one years old, to move to Denver so she and C. J. could begin an extended sales trip to states where there were more black customers.

As they worked their way east, they met great success in Kansas, Oklahoma, Texas, Arkansas,

Louisiana, Mississippi, and Tennessee. They went as far north as New York. At each stop, Sarah demonstrated her Walker System of hair care and trained new Walker sales agents. C. J. helped plan the events. They sent orders for products back to Colorado where Lelia mixed bigger and bigger batches of vegetable shampoo, Wonderful Hair Grower, and Glossine.

Madam Walker would give her clients
manicures while they talked

After a year and a half on the road, they settled in Pittsburgh, where they opened Lelia College of Beauty Culture in the spring of 1908.

Applications came from maids, office cleaners, laundresses, cooks, and even schoolteachers, who all had dreams of making enough money to support themselves without working for someone else. Madam Walker called her graduates "hair culturists" because she believed healing scalp infections and conditioning hair was like "cultivating" a crop.

Madam Walker's Vegetable Shampoo was an improvement over the lye soap that many women used to wash their hair.

Lelia closed the Denver office and joined her mother and C. J. in their office and hair salon on

Pittsburgh's Wylie Avenue. They expanded their mail order operation to supply the hundreds of Walker sales agents they had recruited throughout the Southwestern, Southern, Eastern, and Midwestern United States.

Madam Walker opened her first school in Pittsburgh to train women to become what she called "beauty culturists."

In 1910, the *Pennsylvania Negro Business Directory* featured a half page photograph of Madam Walker and called her "one of the most successful businesswomen of the race in this community." Four years after her first Denver newspaper ad, her appearance had changed dramatically. Posed with her hands clasped behind her back and her hair pinned into a neat twist atop her head, Walker looked confident and serene. Her high-necked, floor-length dress resembled the fashionable clothing she'd admired on others when she was a struggling St. Louis washerwoman.

Between 1906 and 1910, her annual earnings had increased from $1,400 to almost $11,000, or the equivalent of nearly $266,000 in current dollars. At a time when the average white male factory worker was making between $650 and $1300 a year, this was an amazing accomplishment.

Pittsburgh had been a good temporary base, but it lacked some of the assets Madam Walker believed she needed to take her business to the next level. For a more permanent headquarters, she had begun to set her sights on Indianapolis, Indiana.

# Chapter 4
# Giving Back

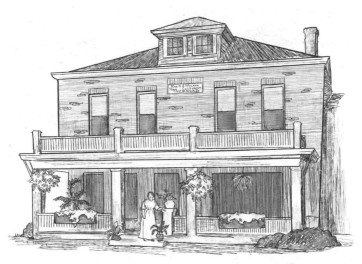

Madam Walker moved her headquarters from
Pennsylvania to Indiana in 1910.

When Madam Walker and C. J. visited
Indianapolis in early 1910, she marveled at
the thriving black business community and its
convenient location. Called the "Crossroads
of America," Indianapolis was a hub for the
extensive highway system then being constructed
for the popular new automobiles. The train
network that brought more than a million freight
cars through the city each year would provide

efficient distribution for her mail order business. With hundreds of passenger trains, she could get to any city in America in less than a week.

During her first trip to the Hoosier capital, Walker met Dr. Joseph Ward, who owned a small hospital, and *Indianapolis Freeman* publisher George Knox, whose newspaper was one of the nation's most widely read black weeklies. They urged her to consider Indianapolis as the base for her business.

Knox also introduced her to a young attorney, Robert Lee Brokenburr, a native of Virginia who had graduated from Hampton Institute and Howard University's School of Law. In September 1911, he filed the articles of incorporation for the Madam C. J. Walker Manufacturing Company to "manufacture and sell a hair growing, beautifying and scalp disease-curing preparation and clean scalps with the same."

Walker persuaded another young attorney, Freeman Briley Ransom, to join her enterprise as her primary legal counsel. Born in Grenada, Mississippi in 1882, he had graduated from

The Madam C. J. Walker Manufacturing Company opened a new factory, school and beauty salon in Indianapolis.

Walden College in Tennessee and taken classes at Columbia University School of Law. Because she traveled so much, Walker realized she needed someone to manage the office while she was away. Ransom's legal skills and even temper were an added bonus. His official title was General Manager, but he filled many roles, including chief legal counsel, chief operating officer, and chief financial officer.

With confidence that the day-to-day operations were firmly under control, she could concentrate on her vision for her company's future. She knew the importance of recruiting other talented employees and building a strong team. In Kentucky, she met Alice Kelly, dean of girls at Eckstein Norton Institute, a boarding school for black children. Impressed with Kelly's

Alice Kelly left her job as dean of girls at a Kentucky school to become manager of the Walker Company factory.

decisive, assertive manner, Walker offered her a position as supervisor of her Indianapolis factory.

The more successful Walker became, the more she focused on self-improvement. She knew making money was not enough to be truly successful. She was aware that her lack of formal education could become a problem in the long run. She very much wanted to polish her speaking and writing skills. So she asked Kelly for advice on social etiquette, penmanship, grammar, and vocabulary. Acting as both traveling companion and tutor, Kelly often joined Walker on sales trips.

Walker also knew how to create promotional campaigns and appealing messages. The daily mail included orders from all over the United States from people who had seen her newspaper advertisements. She put her profits back into her business, expanding her factory, purchasing a second building, and hiring more employees.

Within a year, she could see the results. She had 950 agents nationwide and a monthly income of more than $1,000. Just two years later, she would be earning $1,000 a week.

Madam Walker provided jobs for dozens of office and factory employees as well as thousands of sales agents.

Always serious about her work, Walker also made time for cultural activities and entertainment. She became a patron of the arts, hosting concerts and poetry readings. She commissioned paintings by promising artists and paid for music lessons for young harpists and vocalists. After a day at the office, she often went to the theater to watch silent movies or went home to read books in her library. She hosted dinners and spent evenings with friends listening to recorded music on her Victrola and playing Flinch, a popular card game of the day.

Walker believed it was important to participate in civic activities. She joined Bethel AME Church and supported neighborhood charities. She became particularly interested in the fundraising campaign for the YMCA. George Knox, chairman of the board of the black Indiana Avenue branch, had invited her and other community and business leaders to a meeting to discuss the need for a new building.

Madam Walker contributed $1,000 to help build a YMCA for Indianapolis's black community because they were not welcome at the white YMCA.

Walker believed supporting this effort would help provide recreation and education for children as well as lodging for young men who had come to the city to work.

Jesse Moorland, one of the national YMCA's first black executives, had persuaded Julius Rosenwald, president of Sears, Roebuck and Company, to pledge $25,000 to any city in America where the black and white communities would work together to raise the balance of $75,000 for a $100,000 facility. Such a drive already had been successful in Chicago.

In late October, two wealthy white Indianapolis businessmen kicked off the drive with a $5,000 gift and a $10,000 gift. The next day at a large rally, Madam Walker pledged $1,000. At first the crowd was shocked. No black women ever had contributed that much money to a YMCA.

"If the Association can save our boys, our girls will be saved, and that's what I'm interested in," she said to much applause and foot-stomping. "Some day I would like to see a colored girls' association started."

Ten days later, the city reached its $75,000 goal.

In the process, Madam Walker had made a name for herself beyond the customers who bought her products. Headlines in publications across the country praised her generosity and called her the "Best Known Hair Culturist in America."

Madam Walker was the first
African American woman to own a car

In the midst of this success, however, Walker began to have serious clashes with her husband

C. J. about control of the company and plans for its expansion. Their business differences spilled over into their personal life, finally resulting in a decision to end the marriage. Sarah Walker filed for divorce in late 1912.

# Chapter 5
# On My Own Ground

Madam Walker had made her donation to the YMCA because she believed in the cause. But there were other benefits.

Now, when she gave speeches, she often drew standing room-only crowds. People were curious to learn how she had changed from a washerwoman into an entrepreneur. They were inspired. They also hoped some of her success would rub off on them.

The National Negro Business League held annual conventions for black bankers, publishers, pharmacists, realtors and other entrepreneurs.

During the summer of 1912, Walker gave lectures and promoted her business at black religious, fraternal, and civic conventions along the East Coast and upper Southern states.

Booker T. Washington was the principal of Alabama's Tuskegee Institute and founder of the National Negro Business League.

In July, she arrived in Chicago for the National Negro Business League (NNBL) Convention with hopes of sharing her story with more than 200 black entrepreneurs. These bankers, pharmacists, undertakers, restaurant owners, and inn keepers had come from all over the country. But first she had to convince Booker T.

Washington, the group's founder, to grant her some time at the podium.

Earlier that year, when Walker had visited Washington's Tuskegee Institute, he had not been very welcoming. In fact, he had been rather stiff and less than enthusiastic about her presence on his campus. This time, she was determined to win him over.

On the first day of the convention, Walker paid close attention to one inspiring story after another. Massachusetts real estate broker Watt Terry talked about the steady growth of his business. After selling one house, he used the profits to buy two more. His investments had paid off so well that he now owned fifty houses and two apartment buildings worth half a million dollars.

Walker was even more fascinated by the presentation from Anthony Overton, whose Overton Hygienic Manufacturing Company of Chicago was described as "the largest Negro manufacturing enterprise in the United States." During the previous year, he had sold $117,000 worth of cosmetics, face powder, and baking powder. As Overton was returning to his seat, Washington asked for questions and comments from the audience. George Knox, Walker's Indianapolis colleague, stood up.

George Knox was publisher of the *Indianapolis Freeman*, a newspaper that carried Madam Walker's advertisements.

"I arise to ask this convention for a few minutes of its time to hear a remarkable woman," he said. "She is Madam Walker, the manufacturer of hair goods and preparations."

His request seemed a perfect follow up to Overton's remarks, but Washington ignored Knox even though they had known and respected each other for many years. To make matters worse, Washington called upon another Indianapolis businessman, whose uniform-making company was not far from Walker's factory.

She was terribly disappointed and couldn't help but think that Washington meant to be unkind by not calling on her. She suspected he looked down on her line of work. This made her even more determined to share her story with the delegates and to explain her plans to provide jobs for other women.

The next morning, on the final day of the convention, she waited patiently as several committee reports were presented. When it became clear that Washington had no intention of acknowledging her, she sprang to her feet and spoke in a strong, forceful voice.

"Surely you are not going to shut the door in my face," she declared. "I feel that I am in a business that is a credit to the womanhood of our race. I started in business seven years ago with only $1.50."

Madam Walker shared her inspiring life story with the delegates at the National Negro Business League convention in Chicago.

The audience looked at the forty-four-year old businesswoman with astonishment. Few people had the courage to challenge Washington, a politically powerful person who had been the first black man to be invited to dine in the White House.

"I am a woman who came from the cotton fields of the South," she continued. "I was promoted from there to the washtub."

These words caused some snickering, because many people looked down on women who washed other people's laundry. But Sarah was not ashamed.

"Then I was promoted to the kitchen and from there I promoted myself into the business of manufacturing hair goods and preparations.

"I have built my own factory on my own ground."

Now admiration replaced the audience's laughter.

"My object in life is not simply to make money for myself or to spend it on myself," Walker said. "I love to use a part of what I make in trying to help others."

That evening, Walker's unscheduled speech was the talk of the convention. Delegates clustered around her after dinner, eager to hear more about this newcomer with the dignified manner and firm beliefs.

Walker told them she believed that more women should strike out on their own. "The girls and women of our race must not be afraid to take hold of business endeavors and wring success out of a number of business opportunities that lie at their very doors," she said.

Some of the men disagreed. Their wives, they said, should stay at home to care for their children and do domestic chores. Walker had no interest in debating this issue. From her own experience as a widow and single mother, she knew that many black women had no choice but to work. Either that or they would starve and be homeless. Many married black women needed additional income because some factories and companies preferred to hire white men rather than black men in the kinds of skilled labor occupations and office jobs that paid well.

Black women earned less than any other group of employees in America. Walker remembered the time in her life when she had made less than $2 a week. Now her sales agents were able to earn $10, $20, and even $50 a week.

As the convention ended, Walker believed she had begun to gain Washington's respect. He could not help but notice how others had responded to her message.

In 1913, Madam Walker visited the Washington, DC studio of Addison Scurlock, a famous African American photographer, and took this iconic photograph.

Several months later, he accepted her invitation to be a guest in her home during the

festivities for the opening of the Senate Avenue
YMCA. When his train arrived at Indianapolis's
Union Station after midnight, her chauffeur was
waiting for him.

Madam Walker joined Indianapolis business
and political leaders to welcome Sears Roebuck president,
and others, to the city.

At the dedication ceremony, Washington and
Walker shared the stage.

"This building," he told the 1,200 guests,
"should mean less crime, less drink, less gambling,
and less association with bad characters, and

should make our young men more industrious, more ambitious, and more economical."

Walker could not have been more pleased when Washington took a moment during his speech to acknowledge her $1,000 contribution and to praise her for establishing "a business we should all be proud of."

# Chapter 6
# Harlem Activism

Every morning's mail brought envelopes filled with money orders and dollar bills. Some were crisp and carefully folded. Others were crumpled and soiled. Customers from as far away as Havana, Cuba and Los Angeles, California sent requests to the Indianapolis factory for tins of Madam Walker's Wonderful Hair Grower.

Lelia was also doing a brisk business in Pittsburgh, where she shipped orders to agents in the eastern United States from Massachusetts to Maryland. After three years of running the office, she had noticed a clear trend. At the end of each month, when she looked at state-by-state sales, New York always had the highest volume.

Each time she visited New York City, she found more reasons to want to stay. She loved the energy and the crowds. With five million residents, it was by far America's most populous city. New York claimed the world's tallest buildings and an underground train system that ran all day and all night. People from all over the world lived in neighborhoods called Little Italy, Chinatown, and Greenwich Village.

Madam Walker's daughter, Lelia, convinced her to build a house and beauty salon in New York City's Harlem neighborhood in 1913.

Lelia's favorite area was Harlem at the northern end of the island of Manhattan. She could see that it was becoming the national center of commerce and culture for African Americans.

She persuaded her mother that moving their east coast office from Pennsylvania to Harlem would be good for business. In the spring of 1913, she purchased a four-story townhouse on 136th Street and Lenox Avenue near one of the area's busiest subway stops. She hired an architect to design a beauty salon, quarters for a second Lelia College of Beauty Culture, and an upstairs residence. The first-floor salon was decorated in soft gray tones with royal blue velvet seat cushions and polished wooden floors. The living quarters were lavishly furnished and included a grand piano and gold harp.

"It is just impossible for me to describe it to you," Walker wrote to Ransom after seeing the remodeled spaces for the first time. "The decorators said that of all the work they had done ..., there is nothing equal to it, not even on Fifth Avenue."

Lelia was very happy that her mother was so pleased. But she also had begun to worry

Attorney Freeman B. Ransom, the Walker Company general manager, led daily operations while Madam Walker traveled.

about her health. During the last year, Walker had worked herself to the point of exhaustion and been diagnosed with high blood pressure. Her doctor had advised her to cut back on her travels, but she had too many tasks she wanted to accomplish to heed his advice.

Lelia thought her mother might slow down if she moved to New York. She tried to convince her that Ransom and Alice Kelly could handle the day-to-day office and factory operations while she focused on strategy and future planning.

Finally, in 1916, Walker agreed to live in Harlem with Lelia as long as she could get regular reports from Indianapolis. She also had decided that she wanted to be more involved in national political causes and New York's cultural activities.

Harlem welcomed Madam Walker with flattering headlines. Within weeks of her arrival, she was featured on the cover of the *Colored American Review*. Another local paper hailed her as a woman who "has risen to command the respect of tens of thousands of both races" and "an inspiring example to girls and women."

Walker arrived at the same time that many black Southerners and Caribbean immigrants were joining a great migration to America's northern cities. Families from Georgia, Alabama, South Carolina, North Carolina, and Virginia were escaping the South's racial segregation and violence.

With the New York office now open, the Walker women were in a perfect position to train some of the newcomers. Enrollment at Lelia College mushroomed.

Jobs in Pittsburgh's steel mills and Chicago's meat packing plants had been off limits for black men in the past. But after World War I started in Europe in 1914, the number of European immigrants declined drastically. The shortage of workers became even more severe after America entered the war in the spring of 1917. Companies that had refused to hire black men now were desperate for workers because so many men were being drafted into the Army.

But not everyone welcomed them. In some factories, white men resented their presence. They thought they were taking jobs away from other white men. Sometimes there were fights and attacks.

In July 1917, tensions reached a breaking point in East St. Louis, Illinois where black workers and white workers had been in conflict during a yearlong labor strike. In broad daylight, white mobs murdered more than forty black people and seriously injured hundreds more. Homes were burned and businesses destroyed.

After the riots, black citizens throughout America were outraged and grief-stricken. Their anger was even greater because thousands of young black men had shown their patriotism by joining the Army to fight for their country in the war in France. Although a few white political leaders came to their defense, President Woodrow Wilson offered no support or assistance.

In Harlem, Walker met with other leading citizens to discuss how to respond to East St. Louis, as well as to the violence that affected

Angry white workers attacked black residents
in East St. Louis, Illinois to try to force them to leave the city.

hundreds of other communities. They decided that the most effective way to draw attention to the issue was to stage a Negro Silent Protest Parade.

Madam Walker helped organize New York's Silent Protest Parade to protest lynching and racial violence that harmed African Americans.

Shortly after noon on July 28, more than 10,000 black New Yorkers began a somber, purposeful march down Fifth Avenue. The women and children were dressed in white, the men in dark suits. They demanded an end to lynching. The only sound was the roll of muffled drums and the rumble of marching feet. More than 20,000 spectators, who were as silent as the marchers, lined the sidewalks.

Four days after the parade, Walker joined NAACP secretary James Weldon Johnson, *New York Age* publisher Fred Moore, and other Harlem leaders on a train ride to Washington, DC. They planned to present a petition to President Wilson urging him to support legislation to make lynching a federal crime.

They intended to tell him about the 2,867 black men and women who had been lynched in the previous three decades. Because only five people ever had been convicted of these murders, they believed the individual states were either unwilling or unable to prosecute the crimes.

They had been promised an appointment with the President, but when they arrived at the White House, they were told the meeting had been cancelled.

TO THE PRESIDENT AND CONGRESS OF THE UNITED STATES:

We, the committee of the Negro Silent Protest Parade, representing the colored people of Greater New York and the sentiment of the people of Negro descent throughout this land, come to you to present a petition for redress of grievances.

In the last thirty-one years 2,867 colored men and women have been lynched by mobs without trial. Less than a half dozen persons out of the tens of thousands involved have received any punishment whatsoever for these crimes, and not a single one has been punished for murder. In addition to this, mobs have harried and murdered colored citizens time and time again with impunity, culminating in the latest atrocity at East St. Louis where nearly a hundred innocent, hard working citizens were done to death in broad daylight for seeking to earn an honest living.

We believe that this spirit of lawlessness is doing untold injury to our country and we submit that the record proves that the states are either unwilling or unable to put down lynching and mob violence.

We ask, therefore, that lynching and mob violence be made a national crime punishable by the laws of the United States and that this be done by federal enactment, or if necessary, by constitutional amendment. We believe that there can be found in recent legislation abundant precedent for action of this sort, and whether this be true or not, no nation that seeks to fight the battles of civilization can afford to march in blood-smeared garments.

We ask, therefore, immediate action by the Congress and the President of the United States.

Madam Walker and other Harlem leaders traveled to Washington, DC to present an anti-lynching petition to President Woodrow Wilson.

They had not come to Washington expecting miracles. They knew Wilson's views on racial matters reflected the attitudes of the Confederacy and the Old South, where he had been born. Still, they had hoped he would have had the decency to understand the urgency of their message. Extremely disappointed, they presented their petition, left the White House and went to Capitol Hill to meet with a few sympathetic members of Congress.

# Chapter 7

# Women's Duty to Women

Despite her promise to travel less, Walker was unable to sit still. Her mind always was racing with ideas for her business. Instead of slowing down, she had spent much of 1916 and 1917 criss-crossing the United States.

She'd kicked off her tour in North Carolina in March, then made her way through South Carolina and Georgia before spending a week with her friend, Margaret Murray Washington, at Tuskegee Institute in Alabama. During April and May, she continued on to Tennessee, Kentucky, and Indiana. After a few days at home in New York, she was off again to New England where she visited Connecticut, Maryland, and Massachusetts.

At each stop, she organized her agents into local clubs. She gave them instructions for how to conduct monthly meetings and encouraged them to recruit new members.

Her ultimate goal was to bring the women together at a national convention. As she planned, she honed in on three primary objectives. First, she wanted to teach the latest hair grooming practices. Second, she wanted to provide tips to help them increase their sales. Third, she wanted them to understand that contributing to charitable causes was as important to her as their personal earnings and profits.

More than 200 delegates met in Philadelphia in 1917 for the first annual national convention of Walker sales agents and beauty culturists.

In August 1917, a few weeks after her visit to the White House, Walker greeted two hundred well-dressed, and of course well-coiffed, women at Philadelphia's Union Baptist Church for three days of meetings, lectures, and training sessions. They had come from almost every state.

At the time, women and girls rarely traveled to other cities unless they were with their fathers or husbands. Women did not yet have the right to vote in federal elections and very few owned businesses. This convention of the Madam C. J. Walker Beauty Culturists Union was one of the nation's very first formal gatherings of women entrepreneurs.

Walker had seen the power of national organizations and the results they could achieve when their members worked together. She long had admired the NACW and its impact on health, education, and social welfare matters. The NNBL and the NAACP provided helpful examples for convention structure. But she envisioned something new: a national organization of economically successful black women who pooled their financial resources for political and social clout.

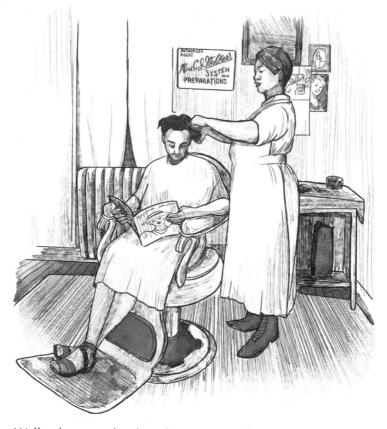

Walker beauty school graduates opened hair salons all over the United States as well as the Caribbean and Central America.

"Nowhere will you find such a large number of successful businesswomen as are among the delegates of this convention," Walker told a reporter.

During the sessions, the delegates described how they had been able to purchase new homes, educate their children and contribute to their churches.

"You have made it possible for a colored woman to make more money in a day than she could in a month working in someone else's kitchen," one woman told her.

Walker was thrilled to hear their stories. She encouraged them by awarding prizes—$500 in all—to the women who had trained the most new agents and who had logged the highest sales. But to emphasize what she called the "benevolent side" of her organization, she presented the largest prizes to the local clubs that had contributed the most to charity and social causes.

In her keynote address—"Women's Duty to Women"—Walker reinforced the message of philanthropy and social uplift.

"I want my agents to feel that their first duty is to humanity," she said. "I shall expect to find them taking the lead not only in operating a successful business, but in every movement in the interest of our colored citizenship."

The Walker System of Beauty Culture allowed many women to start businesses and make enough money to buy homes.

She was especially concerned about the welfare of the migrants who were coming to the cities from rural areas. She knew they had little formal education or understanding of city life. She knew that some people made fun of their country ways. Perhaps she understood what they were going through because she had faced the same negative attitudes when she arrived in St. Louis three decades earlier. But she had been helped and she wanted her agents to feel the same responsibility to others.

"What, I ask, are we going to do about the young boys and girls who find their way into these communities?" she asked. "I tell you that we have a duty to our brother and sister from the South."

"It is my duty, your duty, to go out in the back alleys and side streets and bring them into your home...where they can feel the spirit and catch the inspiration of higher and better living."

Walker also urged the delegates to pay attention to current events and to be politically active. She encouraged them to support

America's troops in France and "to remain loyal to our homes, our country, and our flag."

But after her visit to Washington—and President Wilson's refusal to meet with the Silent Protest Parade leaders—Walker resolved to keep up the pressure.

"We must not let our love of country, our patriotic loyalty cause us to abate one whit in our protest against wrong and injustice," she declared. "We should protest until the American sense of justice is so aroused that such affairs as the East St. Louis riot be forever impossible."

Madam Walker encouraged her employees to be community leaders and to contribute to charity.

At the end of the convention, the Madam Walker Beauty Culturists Union sent a telegram to the White House protesting mob violence and pushing for a federal anti-lynching law.

Walker's dreams for her convention had exceeded her expectations. Now her agents were not only selling hair care products and making money for themselves, they also were positioned to be a force for good.

# Chapter 8
# Her Dream of Dreams

Madam Walker always seemed to have her mind on the next challenge and the next opportunity. Moving to Harlem had put her right where she wanted to be. Now she was in constant contact with political leaders, publishers, and civil rights advocates.

She was very happy to be in the same city as Lelia, but she also had begun to think about building a home of her own where she could entertain friends and host large gatherings.

In late 1916, she bought a large piece of land in Irvington-on-Hudson, a wealthy community twenty miles north of New York City. Railroad mogul Jay Gould's mansion was less than a mile away. John D. Rockefeller's Kykuit, a 300-acre estate, was a few miles up the Hudson River.

She hired Vertner Woodson Tandy, the first licensed black architect in New York State, to design a thirty-four room house. The idea that a woman who had been born in a slave cabin might now own a home in Westchester County was beyond imagination.

Madam Walker moved to New York in 1916 and hired an architect to design a mansion in the village of Irvington.

One of the first stops she made after returning from her convention in Philadelphia was a visit to check on the construction progress. She invited her friend, Ida B. Wells, to ride from Manhattan to Irvington. Walker admired Wells's work as a journalist and an activist who raised awareness about lynching. As Walker's chauffeur drove, the women discussed how they could work together to push for anti-lynching legislation.

"I was one of the skeptics that paid little heed to her predictions as to what she was going to do," Wells wrote as she remembered the first time they had met a decade earlier. "To see her phenomenal rise made me take pride anew in Negro womanhood."

The Italian opera singer, Enrico Caruso, called Walker's new home "Villa Lewaro," using letters from her daughter Lelia Walker Robinson's name.

Several weeks later, Lelia invited Enrico Caruso, the famous Italian singer, to tour the grounds and the gardens. She and her mother both loved opera, so they had attended one of his performances. When he saw the back terrace, he was reminded of homes in his native Naples. On the spot, he suggested that the estate be named Villa Lewaro, using the syllables Le and Wa from Lelia Walker, as well as Ro from Robinson, the last name of Lelia's former husband.

By late spring of 1918, Lelia had helped Walker order linens, silver, china, carpets, and everything she'd need to live in comfort. Antique tapestries and custom furniture had been selected by interior designers. For the dining room, Walker commissioned hand-painted ceilings and installed recessed lighting to create a relaxed atmosphere. The wood-paneled library was stocked with works by great authors from Paul Laurence Dunbar and Mark Twain to Henry Wadsworth Longfellow and Honore de Balzac.

The music room featured two shimmering chandeliers, a grand piano trimmed in 24-carat gold leaf, and an Estey organ with pipes that extended throughout the entire house. A curved marble staircase led to the second level where Walker's master suite offered a view of the Hudson River and sunsets over the New Jersey Palisades.

When Walker moved into the house in June, she described it as "her dream of dreams."

"Every morning at six o'clock, I am at work in the garden, pulling weeds, gathering berries and vegetables," she wrote to Ransom. "You should see me now, all dressed up in overalls. I am a full-fledged 'farmerette.'"

Villa Lewaro's music room was furnished with a harp, a grand piano and an organ that could be heard in the upstairs bedrooms.

She quickly began planning an event to open her home to her friends. She wanted the gathering to be both a celebration and a chance to discuss current events and civil rights.

When America entered World War I in April 1917, there had been a debate about what role African Americans should play in the Army. There were some in the black community who questioned whether black men should be asked to risk their lives in France when they were treated as second class citizens in their own country. Others argued that their patriotism and loyalty would prove to prejudiced whites that black people had an equal stake in the nation's welfare and deserved equal rights.

Walker joined in with a group of black leaders from across the political spectrum who supported this position. Along with W.E.B. Du Bois, editor of the NAACP's magazine, *The Crisis*; NAACP field secretary James Weldon Johnson; Booker T. Washington's former chief of staff Emmett Scott; and others; she pushed for a training camp in Iowa for college-educated black officers. She threw herself into the cause with her usual vigor by visiting military camps to show moral support for black soldiers. She and Lelia raised money for an ambulance through a women's group called the Circle for Negro War Relief.

During World War I, Madam Walker visited military camps to encourage soldiers before they left for the battlefields in France.

To bring attention to all these matters, Walker planned her opening party as a tribute to Emmett Scott. He had been appointed Special Assistant to the Secretary of War for Negro Affairs, and was the highest-ranking black official in the federal government.

Walker invited several prominent black and white civil rights leaders as well as educators, ministers, newspaper reporters, and entrepreneurs. They all were in awe as they got their first look at the entryway's tall white columns, the lush landscaping, and the elegant interior.

Walker's "A Conference of Interest to the Race" featured music and dancing, as well as serious discussion

The weekend featured more than good food, lighthearted conversation, and entertainment by famous musicians. Walker's invitation had billed the event as "A Conference of Interest to the Race."

Scott and some of her other guests made speeches. They discussed and debated serious matters. They were proud of Harlem's 369th Regiment and the unit's achievement as the first Allied troops to reach Germany's Rhine River. But they were extremely concerned that black soldiers were being segregated in training camps at home and given the most menial assignments in France.

After the war, Madam Walker hosted soldiers from Harlem's 369th Infantry Regiment at Villa Lewaro.

They also worried about how the soldiers would be treated once they were back in America. Walker expressed her concern and insisted that they should not face the threat of lynching and "the old order of things."

"Their country called them to defend its honor on the battlefield of Europe," she said. "They will come back to face like men whatever is in store for them and, like men, defend themselves, their families and their homes."

"A Conference of Interest to the Race" was a success and really got people talking

One of her guests, a white military officer, thought she was being too militant, but she and most of her other visitors resolved to stand up for the rights of black veterans if they were attacked.

"It will be a very great pleasure during all the years to come that we were the first official guests entertained at Villa Lewaro," Scott wrote to Walker a few days later. "The wonderful gathering of friends was beyond compare. No such assemblage has ever gathered at the private home of an representative or our race, I am sure."

# Chapter 9
# <u>Legacy</u>

Madam Walker spent much of the summer of 1918 traveling to conferences. At her second annual Walker agents' convention in Chicago, she reminded the delegates that success required extra effort and creativity. "My advice to every one expecting to go into business is to hit often and hit hard," she said. "In other words, strike with all your might."

At the National Negro Business League convention in Atlantic City, she was praised by Vertner Tandy, the architect who had designed Villa Lewaro. He gave her credit for boosting his success at a time when black architects usually were excluded from important construction projects.

But it was in Denver at the National Association of Colored Women's convention where she received one of her most cherished honors. A decade and a half earlier, she had been on the sidelines when the NACW met at her church in St. Louis. Now she was in the spotlight at Shorter AME, the church she had attended while living in Colorado.

Not satisfied just owning a car, Madam Walker became one of the first women to drive her own car

NACW president Mary Burnett Talbert invited her to the stage to thank her for her $500 contribution to the organization's fundraising campaign to buy the Washington, DC home of Frederick Douglass, the famous abolitionist, journalist and orator. As the most generous donor, she was asked to hold a lighted candle that was used to burn a copy of the mortgage. The ceremony was a symbolic act to show the property was free of debt.

Today the home is a National Historic Landmark that celebrates the accomplishments of a man who became president of the Freedman's Bank and influenced President Abraham Lincoln's views on slavery.

After the busy summer, Madam Walker returned to New York to focus on Walker Company business. She and her attorney wrote letters to each other about her plans to expand the factory in Indianapolis. They also exchanged ideas about increasing their national and international sales. Just before Christmas 1918, Madam Walker received dozens of cards from friends and employees as she celebrated her fifty-first birthday. On Christmas Eve, she was joined at Villa Lewaro by a few close friends and special guests she admired. A sculptor named May Howard Jackson was there along with two

Washington, DC, teachers, an AME minister from Baltimore, and three World War I veterans.

After dinner on Christmas Day, the group drove to Harlem for a basketball game at the Manhattan Casino. Walker was greeted with a standing ovation as she entered the gymnasium.

After Madam Walker became wealthy, she helped others because she remembered that people had helped her and been kind when she was poor and homeless.

Early the next morning, she rode with her chauffeur to a pier in lower Manhattan where she joined a delegation of prominent New Yorkers who had been invited to review the return of the Atlantic Fleet from the war in Europe. At Mayor John S. Hyland's invitation, she boarded a small boat that motored into New York harbor for a closer look at the warships as they passed the Statue of Liberty.

Two weeks later, Attorney Ransom informed her that her 1918 sales had topped $275,000, or $4.8 million in today's dollars. The Madam C. J. Walker Manufacturing Company had become one of the most successful black-owned and women-owned companies in America. Walker was well on her way to becoming a millionaire.

She took a moment to savor the news. But, as always, there was more work to do. She was busy approving the design for packaging for her new line of skin care products. Lelia needed her help to prepare for a trip to Panama, where she would train sales agents and expand their business in Central America. Walker already was beginning to line up speakers for her third annual convention in August.

Financially, the outlook could not have been better, but her hypertension had gotten worse. Once again, her doctor pleaded with her to get more rest.

Indeed, she had not traveled since late summer, but she could not resist the chance to spend the upcoming Easter holiday in St. Louis with her old friends Jessie and C.K. Robinson. Jessie, who once had been her mentor, now was one of her leading sales agents and beauty culture instructors.

Walker told herself that she would do more relaxing than working. Before Lelia left for Panama, Walker had promised that she would make only one speech while visiting her former hometown.

On Easter Sunday, just as Walker was getting dressed for services at St. Paul AME, she collapsed. The Robinsons called their family doctor, who delivered troubling news. Walker's blood pressure had spiked so severely that her kidneys were failing. The doctor insisted that she return immediately to Irvington. After reserving a private train car, he and his nurse accompanied her to New York.

After her collapse, Madam Walker met with her attorneys to divide up her money

When they arrived three days later, Ransom was waiting at Villa Lewaro. Walker was physically weak, but mentally strong enough to review her personal affairs and finances.

She advised Ransom to pledge $5,000 to the NAACP's crusade against racial violence. The next day, Mary Talbert, a founder of the NAACP and current NACW president, announced her friend's gift at the NAACP's Anti-Lynching Conference at Carnegie Hall. The 2,500 delegates cheered for several minutes. Walker's contribution was the largest the organization ever had received. A prosperous farmer from Arkansas was so inspired by her generosity that he made his own $1,000 pledge. By the end of the week, an additional $3,400 had been promised in smaller donations.

Madam Walker became a member of the National Association of Colored Women and raised money for its programs.

During the next few days, Walker directed Ransom to set aside $100,000 for more than three dozen organizations, schools, and individuals. Her list included Tuskegee Institute, Dr. Mary McLeod Bethune's Daytona Normal and Industrial Institute for Girls, the St. Louis Orphans home, and YMCAs and YWCAs in four cities. Her daughter Lelia, of course, was to be the primary beneficiary of the rest of her estate.

Madam Walker died in May 1919 and is buried in Woodlawn Cemetery in the Bronx, New York.

Early Sunday morning, May 25—as Lelia was rushing home from Panama—Sarah Breedlove Walker died at Villa Lewaro.

Tributes poured in from all over the nation as well as the Caribbean and Central America. Even newspapers in Paris noted her death. Telegrams sat in stacks on a large table near the front door. Floral arrangements crowded the music room.

Her life was "the clearest demonstration I know of Negro women's ability recorded in history," wrote her good friend, Mary Bethune. "Her work shall live as an inspiration to not only her race but to the world."

"It is given to few persons to transform a people in a generation," W. E. B. Du Bois noted in his *Crisis* obituary. "Yet this was done by the late Madam C. J. Walker. She made and deserved a fortune and gave much of it away generously."

At the time of her death, Walker was considered the wealthiest black woman in America and among the first self-made American female millionaires. Her estate was valued at between $600,000 and $700,000. The estimated value of her company was set at $1.5 million.

Walker was a pioneer of what is now a multibillion-dollar international cosmetics industry. She used the kind of marketing strategies and training systems that still show results. She understood the power of public relations and advertised extensively in the black press.

She was an early champion for working women and a philanthropist who shared her good fortune with others. As a political activist, she understood collective action and urged her sales agents to use their financial clout to protest racial injustice.

Madam Walker will always be remembered as a woman who transformed herself from a poor washerwoman into a successful entrepreneur.

She had the courage to dream and the will to overcome obstacles. Her story continues to inspire others.

Madam Walker appeared on a U. S. postage stamp in 1998.

# Select Quotes from Madam C. J. Walker

"I got my start by giving myself a start."

— *New York Times Magazine*, November 1917

"Now my object in life is not simply to make money for myself or to spend it on myself in dressing or running around in any automobile, but I love to use a part of what I make to help others."

— National Negro Business League Convention, 1912

"I had to make my own living and my own opportunity. But I made it. That is why I want to say to every Negro woman present: Don't sit down and wait for the opportunities to come. You have to get up and make them for yourselves!"

— National Negro Business League Convention, 1914

"We must not let our love of country, our patriotic loyalty cause us to abate one whit in our protest against wrong and injustice. We should protest until the American sense of justice is so aroused that such affairs as the East St. Louis riot be forever impossible."

— 1917 Walker Convention Proceedings

"There is no royal, flower strewn road to success, and if there is I have not found it for whatever success I have obtained is the result of many sleepless nights and real hard work."

— *Indianapolis Recorder*, March 15, 1919

# Madam C. J. Walker Timeline

**1867 Dec 23**  Sarah Breedlove is born in Delta, Louisiana

**1874**  Orphaned at age six when her parents die

**1878**  Moves to Vicksburg, Mississippi with her sister

**1882**  Marries Moses McWilliams

**1885 June 6**  Gives birth to daughter, Lelia (later is known as A'Lelia Walker)

**1888**  Widowed when Moses dies; Moves to St. Louis

**1905**  Moves to Denver and experiments with hair products

**1906**  Marries Charles Joseph "C.J." Walker and founds Madam C. J. Walker Manufacturing Company

**1908**  Moves to Pittsburgh and opens Lelia College

**1910**  Moves to Indianapolis and builds factory

**1911**  Pledges $1,000 to Indianapolis YMCA building fund

**1911**  Madam C. J. Walker Manufacturing company officially incorporated

**1912**  Travels throughout U.S. training sales agents

**1913**  Expands business in Caribbean and Central America; Opens Lelia College of Beauty Culture in Harlem with her daughter

**1916**  Moves to Harlem in New York City

**1917 August 1**  Visits White House to petition President Woodrow Wilson to support legislation to make lynching a federal crime

**1917 August 31**  Convenes first annual Madam Walker Hair Culturist Union Convention

# World Timeline

**1861 April**    American Civil War begins

**1863 Jan 1**    Emancipation Proclamation becomes law

**1865 April**    American Civil War ends

**1877**    Compromise of 1877 results in withdrawal of federal troops from former Confederate states; Reconstruction ends and Jim Crow laws prevail

**1896 May**    Supreme Court upholds "separate but equal" racial segregation in public facilities as constitutional in Plessy vs. Ferguson case

**1896**    National Association of Colored Women is founded by a group of African American women protesting an offensive publication

**1900**    National Negro Business League is founded by Booker T. Washington

**1909**    National Association for the Advancement of Colored People is founded after 1908 Springfield, Illinois race riot

**1912**    Woodrow Wilson elected president

**1913 March**    Woman Suffrage Parade in Washington, DC protests that women should have the right to vote

**1914**    World War I begins in Europe

**1917 April 6**    America declares war on Germany; enters World War I

**1917 July 2**    East St. Louis Riot

# Madam C. J. Walker Timeline (cont.)

**1918 May**   Moves into Villa Lewaro, her Hudson River estate

**1918 August**   Hosts Emmett Scott at "A Conference of Interest to the Race" at Villa Lewaro

**1919 May**   Contributes $5,000 to NAACP's anti-lynching fund.

**1919 May 25**   Dies at Villa Lewaro; Leaves $100,000 to charitable causes in her will

**1976**   Villa Lewaro designated a National Historic Landmark

**1998**   Becomes twenty-first person honored in U. S. Postal Service's Black Heritage Stamp Series

**2016**   Madam C. J. Walker Beauty Culture hair care line launches at Sephora

# World Timeline (cont.)

**1917 July 28**   Negro Silent Protest Parade on New York's Fifth Avenue

**1918**   Influenza epidemic kills 20 million people worldwide

**1918 November 11**   World War I ends

**1976**   America celebrates it's 200th birthday

**1997 September 15**   Google is registered as a domain name

**2000 November**   Barack Obama is elected the first African American President of the United States

**2016**   President Barack Obama visited Cuba as the first President to do so since 1928

# Glossary

**Ailments**   A bodily disorder or pain

**Antebellum**   In the United States, a period of time between the adoption of the Constitution and the American Civil War

**Astonishment**   Great wonder or surprise

**Bayou**   Marshy body of water, usually found in the south

**Beauty Culturist**   Madam C J Walker used this term to refer to the women trained to use her products

**Cholera**   Disease that causes severe vomiting and diarrhea

**Civil War**   War between the Union in the North and the Confederacy in the South about slavery

**Cotton Bolls**   Capsule of cotton seeds held together

**Cotton Gin**   Machine that separates seeds, hull, and other materials from cotton

**Emancipation Proclamation**   Presidential proclamation that freed all slaves in all states still in the Union

**Entrepreneur**   Someone who organizes, and operates a business or businesses

**Etiquette**   Rules about the proper way to behave

**Great Migration**   Movement of 6 million African Americans out of the rural South and into the Northeast, Midwest, and West from 1916 to 1970

**Harlem**   Large neighborhood in northern Manhattan; home to a major artistic revolution in the 1920s and '30s

**Hoosier**   A resident of the state of Indiana or someone from Indiana

**Hypertension**   Abnormally high blood pressure

**Immigrant**   A person who moves to a new country to live permanently

**Jim Crow Laws**   Laws in the South, both formal and informal, that discriminated against non-white people

**Ku Klux Klan**   Racist group against African American, Catholic, or Jewish people

**Lynching**   to kill without a trial for an unproven crime

**Migrant**   A person who moves to a new place; similar to immigrant except not to a new country

**New England**   The geographic section of the United States containing Connecticut, Maine, Massachusetts, New Hampshire, Rhode Island, and Vermont

**Ointment**   A greasy medicine for use on the skin

**Petrolatum**   An ointment or grease used in many beauty products, similar to petroleum jelly

**Philanthropy**   Charitable acts or gifts to help other people

**Podium**   A small platform on which a person stands to be better seen by an audience

**Reconstruction**   The United States Government's reorganization of the Confederate states after the Civil War from 1895 to 1877

**Salve**   A healing ointment

**Silent Protest Parade**   Protest march in New York City of 10,000 African American people in response to the East St. Louis Massacre

**Sharecroppers**  A farmer who tends someone else's crops and receives a share of the value of the crop minus cost of seed, tools, housing, and food

**Siege of Vicksburg**  Battle that allowed Union soldiers to capture Vicksburg, Mississippi and take control of the Mississippi River

**Sulfur**  A nonmetallic element used in medicine for treating skin diseases

**Tresses**  Long hair that is not tied back in a braid, ponytail, or bun

**Victrola**  A brand of record player

**Washerwoman/Laundress**  Woman who is paid to wash other people's clothes and laundry

**Yellow Fever**  Infectious disease that causes fever, headache, muscle ache, vomiting, and skin yellowing

**YMCA**  Young Men's Christian Association. An organization promoting charity and helping people better themselves in spirit, mind, and body

# Bibliography

Bundles, A'Lelia. *On Her Own Ground: The Life and Times of Madam C. J. Walker.* New York: Scribner, 2001.

Peiss, Kathy. *Hope in a Jar: The Making of America's Beauty Culture.* New York: Metropolitan Books, 1998.

## Further Reading

Giddings, Paula. *When and Where I Enter.* New York: William Morrow, 1984.

Rooks, Noliwe M. *Hair Raising: Beauty, Culture and African American Women.* New Brunswick, N.J.: Rutgers University Press. 1996.

Wells-Barnett, Ida B. *Crusade for Justice: The Autobiography of Ida B. Wells.* Edited by Alfreda M. Duster. Chicago: University of Chicago Press. 1970.

# Index

# Index (cont.)

# Index (cont.)

# Index (cont.)

# Index (cont.)

# Index (cont.)

# Index (cont.)

# Index (cont.)